WHATEVER YOU CHOOSE TO BE

8 Tips for the Road Ahead

ANN ROMNEY

SHADOW
MOUNTAIN

Visit us at ShadowMountain.com

Library of Congress Cataloging-in-Publication Data

Romney, Ann, 1949– author.

Whatever you choose to be : 8 tips for the road ahead / Ann Romney.

pages cm

Text of a commencement address given on May 2, 2014 at Southern Utah University.

Includes bibliographical references.

ISBN 978-1-62972-014-2 (hardbound : alk. paper)

1. Conduct of life. 2. Baccalaureate addresses—Southern Utah University.

I. Title.

BJ1589.R66 2015

170'.44—dc23   2014044952

Printed in the United States of America

Publishers Printing, Salt Lake City, UT

10   9   8   7   6   5   4   3   2   1

FOREWORD

MITT ROMNEY

I have to tell the truth: it wasn't Ann's intellect that first attracted me to her. She was simply the most beautiful girl in the room. She had come to the dance with another guy. I approached him with an offer: "Because I live closer to Ann than you do, why don't I give her a ride home for you?" His agreement sealed one of the best deals I've ever made.

That was almost fifty years ago. Today, she's still the most beautiful girl in the room, but she's also the most impressive. I watch her speak to audiences of all kinds, guide charities to new and more productive courses, and champion new avenues of medical research. At the 2012 Republican Convention, she was the standout. She combines unique insights and wisdom with empathy and charm. I'm profoundly impressed with the woman I love.

Ann's life has been a combination of blessings and challenges. She grew up in a loving home, obtained a college degree, served in her church, and raised a family of five rowdy boys. It seemed like a charmed life. But in 1998, she was diagnosed with multiple sclerosis. Through medical treatment, vigorous exercise, reflexology, blessings, and prayer, she has pushed her disease into remission. Now, with her founding of the Ann Romney Center for Neurological Research, she has gone from one of the wounded to one of the warriors.

Her writings in this book capture some of the lessons from a life that has been lived in full: mother, wife, educator, politician, athlete, first lady of her home state, leader in numerous charities, presidential race campaigner, and best-selling author. Yes, she is all those things, and to me, she is so very much more.

INTRODUCTION

Commencement is both an ending and a beginning. There are so many possibilities and opportunities ahead, with a lifetime of important achievements, exciting adventures, and meaningful relationships. And, perhaps for the first time, the next steps in your life are not set out for you on a predetermined course. For some people, that thought is exhilarating; for others, a little less so. You might feel as if you're a train that's been going full speed ahead and suddenly . . . you're out of track.

I remember how I felt at my college graduation. It was the end of the turbulent sixties and the beginning of the troubled seventies. I was already a new wife and mother. I remember having a clear realization that I had no idea what was next for me. Perhaps you feel that way as well.

It has been said that we live in troubled times. The economy is anemic and good jobs can be hard to find. But this I can tell you with certainty: there is adventure ahead. My guess is that most of us older folks would gladly trade places with you, if we could. At this stage of your life, the future is thrilling and filled with potential.

There is much I could share with you about the road ahead, but I would like to offer eight simple pieces of advice that I wish someone had given to me at my graduation. May God bless you to make the choices that will bring lasting friendships, earned successes, and enduring happiness. A new adventure awaits: whatever you choose to be!

ONE

MAKE YOUR RELATIONSHIPS A PRIORITY

Your friends from college will last a lifetime. On the other hand, I'm sorry to say that much of what you have learned will not.

I took Latin for three years. My dad also took Latin. After all his years of study, he said that he remembered only one simple phrase, which he learned in the first week of class: *Agricola Portat aquam.* Funny thing—after my three years of Latin, you know what I remember? *Agricola Portat aquam.* My kids laughed when I told them that story. But you know what they remember from their Latin? You guessed it: *Agricola Portat aquam.* (Translation: The farmer carries water.)

One of our son's favorite comedy sketches was by Father Guido Sarducci from late night TV. He said he was going to start a five-minute university. In five minutes, he said, you could learn everything that the average college graduate would remember five years after graduation. For example, from his economics course, a student would only need to remember one phrase: *supply and demand.* From his course in business, all you would need to remember was this: buy something and then sell it for more than you paid for it. For Spanish class, he boiled it down to this: *¿Cómo está usted?*

followed by *muy bien*. And by the way, his five-minute university cost only twenty dollars—a real parent pleaser.

In reality, you'll certainly need to remember more than what Father Sarducci predicted, but while your academic lessons grow foggy, your friendships can remain bright. As a new graduate, I imagined that my friends from high school and college would inevitably be supplanted by new people I would meet. How wrong I was! My high school and college friends have brought me a lifetime of association and enjoyment far beyond anything I could have imagined.

For example, Lynn Moon and I played field hockey together and rode horses together. She even went out on a date with Mitt before I did. We've stayed close for over forty years. She and her husband were some of our strongest supporters in our political campaigns.

Your wealth in life will not be measured by your balance sheet because you cannot take it with you in the end. Life's wealth is comprised of the friends and family you hold dear. Do what it takes to keep your relationships alive and well.

Life's wealth

IS COMPRISED OF

the friends and

FAMILY

YOU HOLD DEAR.

Two

DO
SOMEONE
A FAVOR

If you want to get ahead, if you want to achieve true success, do someone a favor. In fact, do favors for lots of people. Some of the most successful people I know are those who go out of their way to do nice things for other people.

Joe O'Donnell is one of the most successful and powerful people in Massachusetts. Because he got into Harvard on a football scholarship, he figured there was no way he could compete with other Harvard graduates in the business world. But there was something about Joe that *was* unique: he naturally went out of his way to help others.

He would spend hours of his valuable time talking with you when you were in need of counsel, or giving your kids career advice, or making arrangements to help a friend-of-a-friend-of-a-friend's sick baby get in to the right doctor. It didn't matter who you were, Joe would go out of his way to help you. And because of that, today Joe has friends from presidents to janitors.

Going out of your way to help other people is simply applying the golden rule: treat others as you want to be treated. It will make you feel good, and it may also lead to earning some gold.

It shouldn't come as a surprise that doing a favor for someone can boost a person's career prospects—that, after all, is the logic behind companies inviting clients to sporting events. What is distinctive about Joe and people like him is that he genuinely enjoys doing things for others and has made it an integral part of his life. My brother Jim is just like that. As an ophthalmologist in San Diego, he has seen his practice thrive not only because of his skill as a surgeon but also because of the heartfelt concern and affection he shows for virtually everyone he knows, including his patients. He listens with rapt interest as his cataract patients regale him with stories about their grandchildren. He personally welcomes patients back to his clinic as though they are best friends, and he volunteers to help them with their special needs.

Jim's kindness extends beyond his professional interests. Several years ago, he heard that a girl in his church congregation who was afflicted with advanced cystic fibrosis needed a transplant. Jim volunteered to be tested, and when it was determined that his tissue was a match, he donated a

lobe from his right lung to her. After the surgery, Jim re-
called, "Looking through the glass at Jennifer, smiling and
sitting up in a chair—well, it was an unbelievable feeling."
Fifteen years on, the girl thrives because of Jim's amazing
gift of life. The more he gives, the more he cares for others,
and the more his own life has been enriched.

GOING OUT OF YOUR WAY

to help people is simply applying

THE GOLDEN RULE:

treat others as you want to be treated.

THREE

DO YOUR
PRESENT JOB
WELL

My father-in-law, George Romney, was one of the most successful businessmen in America. He was also a three-term governor and member of the president's cabinet. This was the advice he gave to young people starting out: Don't worry about a promotion or fixate on what comes next. Instead, do the job you've got as well as you possibly can.

In 1939, George took a job in Detroit as the head of the Automobile Manufacturers Association (now the Alliance of Automobile Manufacturers). He hoped the position would give him insight into the automotive industry, perhaps leading to a midlevel position in a car manufacturing company. But shortly after he took the job, the United States entered the Second World War and the auto companies ceased producing cars in order to manufacture military equipment and aircraft. George was given the responsibility of coordinating wartime production among the five major auto companies. Like millions of other Americans during this time, he put his career aspirations on hold, put his head down, and simply went to work. He did his job so well that when the war was over, one car manufacturer offered him a vice presidency. Another car manufacturer offered him a position as president.

It may come as a surprise that working on a political campaign is far from a cushy, high-status job. Desks are shared, space is cramped, and pay is modest at best. That said, some highly capable young people sign on to a campaign for the experience. And those who go to work—who don't chafe about the pay and the hours, and who excel at whatever job they're given—really stand out.

During Mitt's 2012 presidential campaign, Garrett Jackson signed on as Mitt's "body man." Not a very prestigious job or title. In addition to providing security and running interference in a crowd, Garrett arranged for things like Mitt's peanut-butter sandwiches and the towels he used to wipe off the perspiration. He did his job so well—never complaining, never losing his cool, always being gracious to people around him—that when the campaign was over, one of the campaign finance chairmen hired Garrett into one of the most selective and sought-after private sector positions in the field of finance.

I know there are self-help books that tell you to plan

every step of your career. That may work for some people. But Mitt and I lived by his dad's counsel. We never could have imagined where our life's course would lead—we simply did the very best we could in the job at hand.

Don't worry about a promotion

or fixate on what comes next.

Instead,

DO THE JOB YOU'VE

GOT AS WELL AS YOU

POSSIBLY CAN.

Four

REMEMBER THAT PARENTING IS THE MOST IMPORTANT THING YOU'LL EVER DO

Parenting is probably the most important thing you'll do in life—and the hardest. Too often, young people put off parenting, thinking they can't have both a career and a family. I believe you should make time to be a parent, as it will teach you to truly serve others and work for something and someone beyond yourself.

During Mitt's campaign for governor, he decided that he would spend one day a week doing someone else's job. He worked in an emergency room, he worked on a farm, he cooked sausages at Fenway Park, he loaded garbage on a garbage truck, he laid asphalt for a parking lot, and he worked in a day-care center. After it was all over, I asked him which job was the hardest. Without hesitation, he said that far and away the hardest job was working in the day-care center.

When Mitt and I had a young family and were living in Boston, we were asked to speak with three other couples at Harvard Business School. The topic for the event was how each of us, men and women, had chosen our respective careers. When Mitt told me he had accepted the invitation, my heart sank as I realized that all the other women on the program would be speaking about their high-powered jobs in business and finance. In that setting, I was a little worried about how to present my decision to have a career as a mother.

As I thought about it and began to prepare my talk, I decided that the only thing I could do was to be very honest and speak completely from my heart. The decision to be a full time mother was a career choice that was not highly esteemed by the world, but it was one that I felt very strongly about. I prayed to have the clarity of vision and voice to express myself to this group in an open and loving way.

Fast-forward to the event. It was a large audience, and Mitt and I were the last couple to speak. Just as I had guessed, the other women on the program were highly successful in their professions and held prominent positions in large companies. After the first six speakers, it was Mitt's turn. Everyone in the room knew how successful Mitt Romney had been in his career choices. It was more than a little intimidating. As the final speaker of the evening, I stood with shaking knees and spoke from my heart about what it was like to choose a career as a mother. I talked about both the challenges and the joys of being a mother. I talked about how much I appreciated Mitt's support and his long-term perspective. Mitt would often say that his career was temporary—necessary and good, but temporary—while my career was a permanent, lifelong calling. While I received no worldly recognition for the more grueling path I had chosen, I knew he valued what I was doing and understood it was the thing that mattered most for our family.

I truly expected to be booed for my speech. Instead, I received a standing ovation because the message had resonated with those in the audience who had a mother or father who also recognized the value of having someone in the home. Close to a dozen people approached me afterward and expressed how moved they had been.

Years later, several women reached out to let me know that my remarks had changed the course of their lives—that despite the fact that they had a degree from Harvard Business School, being a mother was more important to them. They had still pursued professional careers, but they had done it in such a way that mothering had become the predominant role. They'd had to make tough decisions, but they were happy with the path they had taken.

Parenting is dirty diapers and sleepless nights, but it's also counseling, teaching, doctoring, investing, praying, analyzing—it's as challenging as any job you may choose to do. And it is more rewarding and exhilarating than anything else you can imagine.

Parenting

·•·

IS AS CHALLENGING AS ANY

JOB YOU MAY CHOOSE TO DO.

And it is more rewarding

and exhilarating than anything else

you can imagine.

Five

RECOGNIZE THAT EVERYONE HAS PROBLEMS

As a young married person, I'd sit in class or at church and see all the other folks looking so happy and carefree. I felt that my problems were mine alone. But some years later, I was given the responsibility of counseling and caring for other women in my congregation. And what I found was that almost everyone was carrying a bag of rocks on his or her back.

Everyone is burdened with challenges, so don't judge people too harshly. They are probably carrying a heavier load than you might imagine. And don't feel alone—everyone might not have the same problems as you, but everyone has problems.

It's sometimes easy to feel that there are people who live a charmed life. Without question, some people do in fact escape problems that many others encounter. Mitt and I feel that we have been unusually fortunate in a number of ways. But our experience has also shown us that nearly everyone faces challenges of one kind or another—challenges that strain their hearts and draw them to their knees.

For some years, we attended a congregation of our church that included a disproportionate number of highly successful businessmen, four of whom were corporate CEOs. Most of the congregants were of modest means, and for them it may have seemed that those four very prosperous families had somehow been spared from heartache. They were not. One family had a daughter afflicted with a degenerative disease that ultimately took her life. Another couple agonized as their eldest child separated herself from the church they loved. One family learned that three of their grandchildren had cystic fibrosis, and another couple's grandchild became seriously disabled.

Over the years Mitt and I have had the opportunity of getting to know many people in a variety of circumstances. What has been most revealing is learning of the struggles and challenges that virtually everyone has endured or is currently experiencing. There are business failures, job losses, health crises, marriage struggles, wayward children, untimely deaths, and so forth. Problems are the rule, not the exception. Those who are happiest are those who don't dwell on why they have problems, but instead accept those challenges and move their lives beyond them.

Everyone

MIGHT NOT HAVE THE SAME

PROBLEMS

as you,

BUT EVERYONE HAS

PROBLEMS.

Six

LIVE FOR A PURPOSE GREATER THAN YOURSELF

Live a purpose-driven life. Pastor Rick Warren wrote a national best seller on that topic. His point was quite simple—if you live your life solely for yourself, for good times and fun, your life will be shallow, empty, and unfulfilling. An abundant life is one that is lived for a purpose greater than oneself.

Tom Monaghan got a check for a billion dollars when he sold Domino's Pizza, a company that he started. What people don't know is that he gave virtually all of the money to Catholic charities. But many years before that, when the company first became really successful, he began to buy things—expensive things. He bought scores of vintage cars. He even bought the Detroit Tigers baseball team. What he found was that those things, living for ego and pride and self-gratification, were empty and unfulfilling. You see, Tom was an orphan who had been raised by Catholic nuns, and after realizing that money couldn't buy happiness, he decided to sell all the things he had accumulated, and he devoted himself to his church. And he still does to this day. This, he told us, is what makes him happy.

Other people devote themselves to their university, to their community, to their politics, or to their family.

Living for something greater than ourselves has made all the difference in the world to Mitt and me. In 1998, we were living in Boston. Mitt's business was doing very well, but I wasn't. I had just been diagnosed with multiple sclerosis. My right leg was numb. I was losing my balance and stumbling. I was very fatigued and unable to do much. Beyond anything else, I was frightened. The disease was progressing rapidly, and I had no idea how debilitated I would become.

Then a phone call came from our friend Kem Gardner: Would we consider coming out to run the troubled Salt Lake City Olympics, then mired in scandal? Now, objectively, that was crazy. I was very sick. Mitt was running a successful business. The timing was terrible, and it made no sense at all. And yet, we went. We left everything behind. It was crazy. It was also the best move we ever made because it came with a higher purpose.

The Games were highly successful. We made friends we

will treasure for a lifetime. And I found that the therapy and blessings I received in Utah helped put my multiple sclerosis in remission. In fact, I was able to run the Olympic torch into Salt Lake City just prior to the opening ceremonies.

AN ABUNDANT LIFE

is one that is lived for a purpose

greater than oneself.

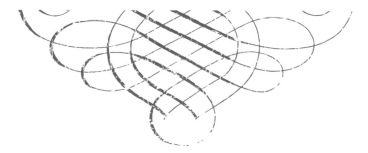

SEVEN

DO SOMETHING YOU LOVE EVERY DAY

Do something you love every day. Take an hour to find joy every day.

When I was a young mother and feeling overwhelmed at times, I learned that it was critical to find time for myself. For me, it was picking up the game of tennis. I absolutely loved it. It got me out of the house for an hour, I got exercise, I made wonderful friends, and I was able to whack the tennis ball instead of whacking the kids. I came home a much happier mother.

When I was diagnosed with multiple sclerosis at age forty-nine, I wondered whether I would continue to be able to do many of things I enjoyed. Everyone's course in a disease like MS is different, but for me, the disease came on fast and strong. My right side became numb. I struggled to climb the stairs, and I was completely exhausted for most of the day. I decided that before I was going to be in a wheelchair, I was going to get back on a horse and ride again. As a girl, I had ridden a horse almost every day, and I loved it. But when I turned fifteen, my dad sold our horse and told me it was time to go out, make friends, and concentrate on my schoolwork. High school and college, then marriage and children, kept me from the daily riding I had loved as a girl.

When the disease struck, I decided that I'd better ride again before I would no longer be able to do so. I showed up at a barn in Heber, Utah, and the staff there helped me get up on a wonderful chestnut horse called Buddy. I barely hung on for a couple of turns around the arena, but it was exhilarating. I loved it so much that I made it a point to get to that barn every day. Modern medicine, reflexology, prayer, and perhaps even those horses helped me regain strength. Now I ride regularly, and with a good deal more skill than I did as a young girl. I'm convinced that having something every day to look forward to not only brightened my spirits but also helped me heal.

Find something you love—cultivate it—and your life will be richer.

Do something you LOVE every day.

EIGHT

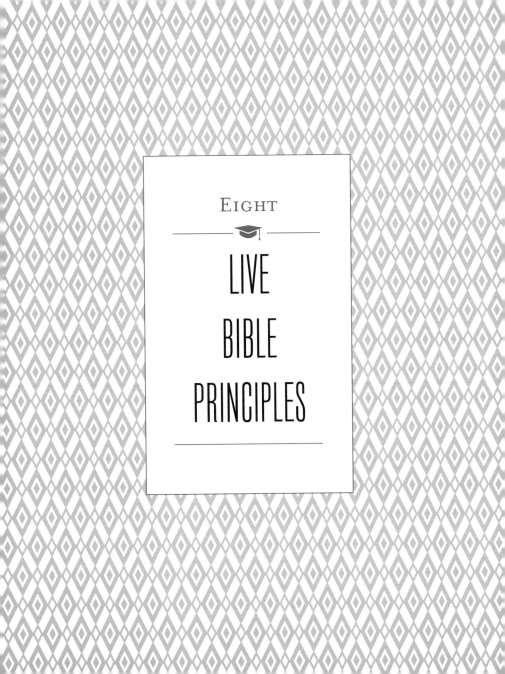

LIVE
BIBLE
PRINCIPLES

The Bible works, so do what it says.

You may not believe like I do that the Bible was in-spired by God. But if not, you'd surely have to admit that it was written by some of the greatest philosophers and thinkers in history. Either way, it's worth paying a good deal of attention to what it has to say. And what I've learned is that following what it says makes life better, happier, more fulfilling, and more abundant.

The Bible tells us to leave our parents' home and to cleave unto our spouse. Your parents will wholeheartedly agree with that one. As a matter of fact, it used to be that the American dream was to own your own home. Now, the American dream is to get your kids out of the home you own.

The Bible tells us that to find ourselves we must lose ourselves in the service of others. Over my lifetime, I have known some very unhappy people. I've found that the best cure for unhappiness is going out and doing something for someone else.

The Bible tells us not to love money, and it gives us a way to help make sure our priorities are in the right place. When Mitt got his first salary, we paid tithing to our church. The check Mitt wrote was so large I cried for joy that we were able to give so much. I think Mitt also cried, but for a different reason.

And the Bible records the admonition of Paul, "Whatsoever things are true, whatsoever things are honest, whatsoever things are just, whatsoever things are pure, whatsoever things are lovely, whatsoever things are of good report; if there be any virtue, and if there be any praise, think on these things" (Philippians 4:8). If you live by that charge, you will enjoy the sublime serenity and peace that Paul experienced.

The lessons taught in the Bible and the gospel of Jesus Christ are meant for you, and for your happiness here and now.

FOLLOWING BIBLE PRINCIPLES

makes life

BETTER,

happier,

MORE FULFILLING,

and more abundant.